Young Men Breaking Free:

12 Steps to Sexual Purity for Young Men

Stephen Wood

Family Life Center Publications

Copyright © 2014 Family Life Center Publications

All rights reserved. No part of this book may be reproduced or transmitted in any form or by any means, electronic or mechanical, including photocopying, recording or by any information storage or retrieval system, without permission in writing from the publisher.

ISBN: 978-0-9821666-0-4

Library of Congress Control Number: 2013955358
Book production: Family Life Center Publications
Cover and layout design: 5sparrows.com
Manufactured in the United States of America

Unless otherwise indicated, Scripture quotations are taken from the Revised Standard Version, Catholic Edition [RSVCE], copyright © 1965 and 1966 by the Division of Christian Education of the National Council of the Churches of Christ in the United States of America. Used by permission.

Family Life Center Publications
2130 Wade Hampton Blvd.
Greenville, SC 29615
www.FamilyLifeCenter.net

Contents

1. Foreword
*Screwtape's Strategies
for Entrapping Young Men*................5

2. 12 Steps to Sexual Purity...............10

3. Appendix
Scripture Memory for a Pure Mind.........47

Resources............................53

Dedicated to
the Memory of Fr. John Mulvey

*A Priest Who Ran to the Front
Where the 21st Century's
Battle Raged the Strongest*

FOREWORD

Screwtape's Strategies for Entrapping Young Men

The Screwtape Letters, a book by C.S. Lewis, unveils a series of secret correspondence between a senior demon, Screwtape, and his neophyte tempter and nephew Wormwood. Lewis uses a type of reverse theology to warn Christians against diabolical temptation strategies. The following account illustrates how Screwtape might utilize the darker sides of the Internet to entrap young Christian men.

My Dear Wormwood:

For your careful review, I have outlined below our strategies for destroying both the faith and future marriages of millions of young men. Destroy this secret message immediately after reading it. This classified material comes from the lowest regions.

In this new millennium, we must bring our master plan to completion by utilizing Internet pornography. Already we have spiritually neutralized millions of the Enemy's men with pornography. Over the next few years we can surely turn millions more into spiritual midgets, whom we can then manipulate at will.

It is most encouraging that Internet pornography has ensnared so many millions of Christian men. These fools think there is no harm in a few swipes on their smartphones, or a few clicks to dirty websites. Little do they know that we can't wait to use their growing porn habit to drive a wedge between them and the Enemy. They'll gradually descend to us as they grow to hate both the Supreme Enemy and even their future spouses. You see, the delightful by-product of pornography addiction is that it is so effective in creating turmoil in those contemptible human relationships. Many young men will not even be interested in pursuing marriage since they have already said "I do" to our virtual delights.

What's more, they'll be buried underneath mountains of their own shame. They will eventually despise their very selves. Their disgrace and humiliation resulting from non-stop porn use will convince them that they are truly unlovable. This is the opportune moment to strike them with condemnation. Subtly confirm their judgment against themselves thereby permanently driving them far away from the Enemy's camp. Any man convinced that he is unlovable is ours and thus immune from any Enemy advances.

When we have finished bombarding them with waves of condemnation, they will call themselves, "Despicable me." Just think. These slimy creatures that the Enemy wanted to exalt and glorify above the angels and archangels are now groveling in the slime of their sin, hopeless of any so-called redemption. Hahahaha!

Of course, spreading the worldwide flood of pornographic images at the speed of light is a vital part of the final phase of our overall plan. The fools still don't realize that the technological temptations are waging war against their very souls, bringing to completion a very long campaign to destroy the Faith. Our goal is to use virtual porn to darken the minds of men so that they can no longer reason properly. Like a rheostat being turned down, their world eventually becomes dark. Just the way we like it.

Be aware that the final pages of the Enemy's book warn them of our virtual strategies to inebriate the world with sexual immorality. That utterly dreadful conclusion of the Enemy's book called Revelation warns of our plans when it says, "The wine of whose fornication the dwellers on earth have become drunk." Some in the Enemy's camp know that the word "fornication" is from the Greek word "porneia" which is a term for all types of sexual immorality. Internet porn has given us the perfect delivery system to bring the modern world into our camp. With the advent of smartphones and tablets the spread of porn is beyond our most diabolical dreams. With abandon, the nations are consuming the wine of impure passion (*porneia*).

By the way, my warning about the closing chapters of the Enemy's book is the only section of my letter that isn't classified since it was revealed over two thousand years ago. There's no need to fear discovery since men don't bother reading that stupid book any more. The

Enemy's book universally collects dust. It's generally more secure than a secret vault.

It is imperative that you scramble any efforts to organize support groups for men. Thwart any attempts to allow young Christian men to gather informally to assist each other in freeing themselves from our work. Just let the poor devils struggle alone — though of course we know that they are not alone in their pornography habit, don't we?

Finally, we must keep up our guard against the Head of THAT family, the man called Joseph. Never forget how the Head of THAT loathsome family was used by the Enemy to ruin our dear servant Herod's plans to kill the so-called Holy One. There are centuries-old rumors from the upper regions that the Head of THAT family will be brought into service at a critical time in history. The last thing we want is a repeat of the first century.

It has taken immense effort, but we have managed to thoroughly confuse modern man (and much of the Church) about the meaning of true manhood and masculinity. We need impure men to continue leading the culture towards our regions. We must keep young men from contact with the Head of THAT family, so that they don't have any effective models of manly purity and righteousness.

Yet we need to be realistic in our strategies. If we cannot keep men away from the Unmentionable One, then at least we can chip away at some of the truth to keep things manageable for us. Keep their beliefs abstract. Men look up to tangible role models. Just be sure they don't discover the Enemy's perfect model for manhood and family life, or our plans will get derailed. We can never hope to lead young men who are devoted to that so-called "Just Man" deeper into the depraved delights of pornography.

Yours diabolically,

Screwtape

12 Steps to Sexual Purity

Here are twelve important steps which, if all are followed, should greatly assist you in breaking or preventing an addiction to pornography:

STEP 1

Destroy All of Your Pornography

Destroy all pornographic picture files, downloaded videos, and all pornographic bookmarks on your smartphone, tablet, and laptop. Rip up any and all porn magazines and put them outside in the trash. Do it right now! You can't "just sort of" want purity and expect to obtain it. You have to make a heartfelt decision to break free of pornography, and then act upon that decision.

Temptations for men usually come through the eyes. Jesus advocates radical steps to rid our lives of anything we look at that would cause us to sin.

> If your right eye causes you to sin, pluck it out and throw it away; it is better that you lose one of your members than that your whole body be thrown into hell. – MATTHEW 5:29

STEP 2

Take Radical Steps to Develop a Protection Plan

The *Catechism of the Catholic Church* teaches, "Sexuality affects all aspects of the human person" (Section 2332). Therefore, if you are under the influence of a life-dominating sexual sin like a pornography habit, you need to take radical steps to reorient your life. You must develop a protection plan in order to avoid the occasions of sin.

First and most important, install a safe browser on each of your Internet connected devices, especially on mobile devices that can cause you to stumble anywhere at any time. See the resource section for suggestions on safe browsers for Internet devices. Take this critical step now!

Second, avoid movies and music that stir up impure thoughts. It's hard enough for a young man with strong physical impulses to maintain sexual purity. Why

12 Steps to Sexual Purity for Young Men

would you view or listen to things that stir up impurities if you really want to quell them? Racy scenes in movies and impure lyrics in music act as "triggers" activating impure thoughts and impulses. Your protection plan should include building a hedge that keeps you from unnecessary trouble.

It's immeasurably easier to avoid movies and media with hot and heavy sex scenes than it is to control your thought life once exposed to impurity in living color on the big screen, or on your tablet. Just tell your friends that you are into sports, a hobby, or the outdoors instead of questionable movies.

Listen to the promptings of the Holy Spirit. If you find that impure thoughts are stirred up while listening to certain types of music, then find alternatives.

> Let us then cast off the works of darkness and put on the armor of light; let us conduct ourselves becomingly as in the day, not in reveling and drunkenness, not in debauchery and licentiousness, not in quarreling and jealousy. But put on the Lord Jesus Christ, <u>and make no provision for the flesh, to gratify its desires</u>.
> – ROMANS 13:12-14

"Making no provision" for trouble is a wise way to avoid it. A protection plan foresees the places, times, events, devices, entertainment, and friends (male and female) that cause you to stumble and allows you to avoid them altogether.

Without a protection plan you are unguarded and vulnerable. Right now is the time to start implementing your protection plan.

> A prudent man sees danger and hides himself; but the simple go on, and suffer for it.
> – PROVERBS 22:3

STEP 3

Confession is Good for Your Heart

The *Catechism of the Catholic Church* says, "the new life in Christian initiation has not abolished the frailty and weakness of human nature, nor the inclination to sin ... which remains in the baptized" (Section 1426). It's no secret that the ultimate point of vulnerability for men is sexual sin.

With stark realism the *Catechism* teaches, "In this battle against our inclination towards evil, who could be brave and watchful enough to escape every wound of sin" (Section 979). Therefore, the Church, like her Savior, knows that in the Christian life forgiveness, cleansing, and restoration are often necessary.

As a baptized man you need to raise your shield against the arrows of condemnation with these scriptures that will strengthen your heart:

> Have mercy on me, O God, according to thy steadfast love; according to thy abundant mercy blot out

> my transgressions. Wash me thoroughly from my iniquity, and cleanse me from my sin!
> – Psalm 51:1-2

> As far as the east is from the west, so far does he remove our transgressions from us. As a father pities his children, so the LORD pities those who fear him.
> – Psalm 103:12-13

Christ by his divine authority and infinite mercy gives his power of forgiveness to priests to absolve sin in the sacrament of Penance. Nothing breaks the power of sin and guilt and turns the tide in the battle for sexual purity like the sacrament of forgiveness.

Let me be blunt: what you absolutely need if you have allowed yourself to form a pornography habit along with its attendant sinful behaviors is a regular habit of confessing your sins in the sacrament of Penance.

Find a priest who takes pornography seriously and regularly go to the sacrament of Penance. Remember, a priest cannot prescribe a cure unless he has all the facts in hand.

You might ask, "What should I do if I keep sinning and need to go again to Confession?" You go! We should never imagine a limitation on Christ's mercy, especially in the sacrament of Penance. The more you need Confession, the more you must go to Confession. There are no excuses and no "buts" ... just get yours to Confession.

Find an Accountability Partner

Small pornography recovery and accountability groups under the direction of parish priests and deacons are crucial for helping men beat their porn habits. If possible, I recommend establishing separate accountability groups: one for young men (teens and single 20-somethings) and another for older and married men. Forming an accountability group is an excellent way to meet one of the most critical needs of contemporary men.

Find at least one accountability partner whom you can call on 24 hours a day if needed. A quick telephone call can help you avoid temptation at vulnerable moments. This telephone strategy is similar to Alcoholics Anonymous, where a person who is tempted to return to alcoholism can call on a friend anytime for prayer and encouragement. Accountability is invaluable in helping you get through times of temptation.

For your initial phase of recovery, it is helpful to have a daily (or even a morning and evening) check-up call from your accountability partner. At a minimum, your friend should ask you every week if you have kept yourself free from sexual sin.

You also need to install software on every mobile device and computer to alert your accountability partner when you stray (see resource section).

Don't be tempted to skip steps 3 and 4. You need the help of a priest and an accountability partner in order to have a realistic hope of breaking your addiction.

Douglas Weiss, himself a recovered sex addict and a nationally-known lecturer on sexual addiction, has stated, "I have not experienced, nor have I met anyone who has experienced sexual addiction recovery *alone*" [emphasis added].

> And though a man might prevail against one who is alone, two will withstand him. A threefold cord is not quickly broken. – Ecclesiastes 4:12

STEP 5

Begin a Life of Daily Scripture Reading

In the largest and most unique survey of its kind in history conducted by the Center for Bible Engagement, Christian men reported being tempted 342 days a year – that's 94% of the days in each year. The temptations relating to sex are 10 times higher than any other of the major temptations men face. Despite being bombarded with sexual temptations, men can find some encouraging news uncovered by this study.

The above mentioned survey found that the statistical probability of Christian men using pornography is 51% lower for men who engage in at least four meaningful contacts with scripture per week. Significantly, those who read scripture only two or three times a week didn't show any statistically significant life change at all, including involvement with pornography.

I need to mention the study found that for teens, the power of four meaningful engagements with scripture didn't show any statistical difference regarding pornography involvement. Why? There's probably a host of reasons. One cause might be the fact that many Christian teens who read the Bible, unwisely overload themselves with sex scenes in movies and other media.

When the Bible tells you to avoid "looking at a woman lustfully" and you go ahead and join your peers in viewing immoral media, then it's probably not surprising that the Bible isn't having its intended effect in helping you guard against pornography.

Another reason is that the teen years are very tough times to maintain sexual integrity. Besides the onslaught of immoral media from every direction, you face raging hormones, scantily dressed girls, sleazy advertising, and a peer culture that proclaims, "If it feels good, just do it."

If you (a teen or twenty-year-old) and I walked down a quiet country road, and you asked me, "What can I do in the midst of today's sewer culture to stay pure?" I'd answer with two verses from Psalm 119:

> How can a young man keep his way pure? By guarding it according to thy word. I have laid up thy word in my heart, that I might not sin against thee. — PSALM 119:9 & 11

My strongest recommendation to any young man who wants to get pure is to *memorize* scripture in addition to reading scripture four-plus times each week. Hiding scripture in your heart is a primary way to gradually be changed from the inside out.

Being a faithful Christian teen or a twenty-year-old today is tough. The way to get strong inside in order to meet this challenge is to memorize, meditate on, and internalize scripture. This is precisely what Jesus did when he used scripture to resist the three attacks of Satan during his forty days in the wilderness. We are living in a highly uncivilized wilderness. Therefore, I urge you to follow Jesus' footsteps and put God's Word deep within your heart.

You might be tempted to give up memorizing scripture after learning a couple of verses. This is where your accountability partner can assist you to move from wanting to memorize scripture to actually doing it.

See the Appendix: Scripture Memory for a Pure Mind, along with the Scripture Memory Kits and the Scripture Computer Program in the resource section.

Many will ask, "What can I do if there's porn rot in my head already?" There isn't a quick and easy way to erase pornography from your mind. It took just a few clicks to get in, but it will take mental discipline to get out.

One cause for the extreme difficulty in erasing pornographic images from the mind is that when men view pornography, a chemical called epinephrine, along with other neurochemicals, is released in the brain. This release of epinephrine causes a deep imprint of the visual image to be stored within the brain. When an act of self-stimulation accompanies the pornography viewing, a surge of epinephrine makes the imprint even stronger. That's why porn images can plague a man for decades.

Rest assured, there is a way out of pornography addiction – but don't fall for the promise of an easy way out.

One of the few effective means of getting these pornographic images out of your head is spending time each day reading and memorizing Scripture. For those of you with real problems in your thought life, it is helpful to read Scripture both morning and evening.

Secular specialists who know about the power of neurochemicals to lodge permanent imprints in the brain are pessimistic about the possibility of dislodging them. In my experience, a disciplined plan of memorizing Scripture *will* clear the rot out of your brain. God has the supernatural ability to thoroughly cleanse his sons, as well as the omnipotent skill to get to parts of the brain unreachable by a surgeon's scalpel to cut out the rot. Carefully consider these two scriptures:

> For he is like a refiner's fire and like fullers' soap; he will sit as a refiner and purifier of silver, and he will purify the sons of Levi and refine them like gold and silver ... — MALACHI 3:2-3

> For the word of God is living and active, sharper than any two-edged sword, piercing to the division

of soul and spirit, of joints and marrow, and discerning the thoughts and intentions of the heart.
– Hebrews 4:12

Be aware that things might appear to get worse when you begin an extensive exposure to Scripture. As the Word of God, coupled with the power of the Holy Spirit, cuts out deeply implanted pornographic images, these subconscious images will surface in your mind. When this happens you are in the initial stages of being cleansed from the inside out.

Don't dare to mentally delight in the rooted-out images that float to your consciousness. Pray at that instant, and use your mental discipline to put them out of your conscious thoughts. Be sure to pray for protection so that these images do not return.

Finally, put your focus on Christ – not on your problems. The most successful drug, alcohol, and pornography addiction recovery programs are those which incorporate a vital faith component. It is extremely difficult to overcome an addiction by a compulsive focus on the problem itself. The addictive appetites need to be redirected to the One who can fulfill our desires with good things (Psalm 103:5).

Reading, meditating on, and memorizing Scripture will assist you in redirecting and transforming both your thoughts and your desires.

STEP 6

Learn to Discern & Combat Spiritual Attacks

Sexual addictions and pornography make one vulnerable to the influence of evil spirits. Before a spiritual attack begins you may be struggling with your own lustful thoughts. Then a spiritual attack launches when a spirit silently intrudes into your mind, adding intensity to your lustful thoughts, or implanting additional ones. You can detect this happening when an ordinary human lust arises and then suddenly erupts into a life of its own, one that seems nearly impossible to dispel.

If an episode of overwhelming lust involves a spiritual attack, you will not be able to shake it with just mental effort alone. It is very easy to get discouraged and feel completely overwhelmed by both lust and the accompanying spiritual assault. Yet you can quickly break the power of the attack by first realizing what is happening, and then by saying a prayer for spiritual protection to your guardian angel and St. Michael the Archangel.

One of the hardest parts in fending off a spiritual attack is learning to recognize when one is happening. Spiritual attacks are covert operations that disguise themselves in order to be successful. Ask God to give you continual discernment. After a spiritual attack is stopped, mental discipline is still needed to control your thoughts.

Also, use sacramentals such as holy water, crucifixes, St. Benedict medals (blessed by a priest with the exorcism prayer), etc. These can be very effective in overcoming or preventing spiritual attacks.

Prayer to St. Michael the Archangel

St. Michael the Archangel, defend us in battle.
Be our defense against the wickedness and snares
  of the Devil.
May God rebuke him, we humbly pray,
and do thou, O Prince of the heavenly hosts,
by the power of God, cast into hell Satan,
and all the evil spirits, who prowl about the world
seeking the ruin of souls. Amen.

I ask everyone ... to recite it [the St. Michael prayer] to obtain help in the battle against forces of darkness and against the spirit of this world.
— BLESSED JOHN PAUL II, AUGUST 24, 1994

STEP 7

You Need Grace – Lots of It

The sacraments, especially the Eucharist, are like rivers of living water that bring fresh strength to your soul. Take advantage of every opportunity to receive grace by frequenting the sacraments.

The sacrament of Penance is the one thing that can break the power of pornography in your life and turn the tide in your battle against pornography. Never allow shame or setbacks to keep you from this sacrament. If you are guilty of serious sin, a good confession is the necessary first step to prepare you for receiving further graces in the Eucharist.

The Eucharist has been called a "fountain of graces." These graces include a deeper union with Christ and an increase in sanctifying grace, thereby strengthening a man's spiritual life. Other effects flowing from Holy Communion include helping to free us from daily faults, preserving our souls from mortal sin, and a lessening of concupiscence, the disordered appetites or desires which produce an inclination to sin.

> The increase of charity is the lessening of concupiscence. – ST. AUGUSTINE

> [The Eucharist] restrains and represses the lusts of the flesh, for while it inflames the soul more ardently with the fire of charity, it of necessity extinguishes the ardor of concupiscence.
> – *The Catechism of the Council of Trent*

A more frequent reception of the Blessed Eucharist will make a vital difference in your life. Remember that you must be free of all grave (i.e., mortal) sin before partaking of the Eucharist. The benefits from Holy Communion will strengthen you in your battle for purity.

STEP 8

Both Vices & Virtues are Strengthened by Practice

An addiction to pornography is never static. It starts with what seems like just a little dabbling in digital lusts. Next you begin searching for more graphic pornography. Before you know it you are hooked on the technological temptations. As your conscience becomes desensitized, the images that were disgusting when you started viewing pornography become enticing. The most dangerous step is when guys try to force girlfriends to act out the porn images.

> The alternative is clear: either man governs his passions and finds peace, or he lets himself be dominated by them and becomes unhappy.
> – CATECHISM OF THE CATHOLIC CHURCH, SECTION 2339

If you are viewing pornography, then your vices have been strengthened by repeated practice, and your corresponding virtues of chastity and purity are very weak. It will take time to reverse this, but the more you practice virtue the easier it will become. Changes resulting from strengthened virtue will give you hope and encouragement to persevere.

Some guys have found that setting a 30 or 40 day goal of no porn reactivates long neglected virtues. Advent and Lent are among the many good times to start getting free of pornography, but the best time to begin is today.

St. Paul said, "We do not lose heart … our inner man is being renewed every day" (2 Corinthians 4:16). The more completely you break with your sexual addiction, the easier it will be to overcome it.

Do realize, however, that it will take time, perseverance, and effort. Yet every time you say, "No" to porn the stronger your virtues become.

> For just as you once yielded your members to impurity and to greater and greater iniquity, so now yield your members to righteousness for sanctification.
> – ROMANS 6:19

It is vitally important to remember that the power to change doesn't come from your unaided self-effort. Personal transformation is the result of the inner working of the Holy Spirit as you labor to advance in virtue.

> …Work out your own salvation with fear and trembling; for God is at work in you, both to will and to work for his good pleasure. – PHILIPPIANS 2:12-13

But I say, walk by the Spirit, and do not gratify the desires of the flesh. Now the works of the flesh are plain: fornication, impurity, licentiousness ... But the fruit of the Spirit is love, joy, peace ... [and] self-control. —GALATIANS 5:16, 19, 22-23

Pray

Pray the Rosary often. In God's plan, the Blessed Mother, in union with her Son, is going to crush the serpent's (Satan's) head (Genesis 3:15). Mary can play a vital role in your life by neutralizing the serpent's venom of pornography.

Sexual sin is like a snowball. Temptations and lustful thoughts generally start slow and small and after a brief time pick up speed and size until they swell into an avalanche destroying the power to resist. St. James describes the process of temptation like this:

> Each person is tempted when he is lured and enticed by his own desire. Then desire when it has conceived gives birth to sin; and sin when it is full-grown brings forth death. — JAMES 1:14-15

Most men can't resist an avalanche of lustful thoughts, but every man can stop a puny snowball just as it begins its downward slope.

Therefore, the most effective way to deal with tempting thoughts is to stop them in their tracks as close to their origin as possible. There are a few supremely effective ways to do this.

The first method is to say a single "Hail Mary" at the precise moment an enticement to sin begins. You need to be as quick with a "Hail Mary" as a skilled fighter delivering a counter punch. You'll become a skilled warrior in the battle for manly purity if you learn to do this with an almost automatic instinct.

The second method is to say the Jesus Prayer. You might ask, "What in the world is the Jesus Prayer?"

The Jesus Prayer is a very ancient prayer that Christians through the centuries have prayed, sometimes hundreds of times a day, in an effort to fulfill St. Paul's exhortation to "pray constantly" (1 Thessalonians 5:17).

The short form of the Jesus prayer is, "Lord Jesus Christ, have mercy on me." Its longer form, which I prefer, is, "Lord Jesus Christ, Son of God, have mercy on me, a sinner."

Let me say something about the power of this prayer. There's tremendous power in the name of Jesus, and each time you say the Jesus Prayer, you're saying his name. You may find yourself strengthened in an area where you were weak. Don't underestimate the power of this prayer.

Praying the Jesus Prayer in addition to the Hail Mary at the initial stages of temptation is the perfect way for you and me to deliver a one-two punch in the battle against temptation.

Catholic schools used to teach students to write, "JMJ" for "Jesus, Mary, and Joseph" on the top of each paper or test to remind them that all of the members of the Holy Family are watching over and praying for them. So, let's not forget to ask for the protection of St. Joseph, the guardian of the Holy Family.

St. Joseph is called the just and righteous man. The Epistle of James says, "The prayer of a righteous man has great power in its effects" (5:16). Thus, St. Joseph can powerfully intercede for every Christian man struggling with pornography. All you have to do is ask for his intercession.

Don't let the enemies of your soul keep you isolated. Ask for the intercessions of the saints. Ask for the intercession of your patron saint. In particular, St. Benedict's intercession is known to be exceptionally powerful against wicked spirits.

Another wise step is to ask a contemplative religious order to pray for you in their daily intentions (cf. James 5:16). Remarkable answers to prayer result from the intercessions of a holy religious order.

Developing a regular prayer life fosters integrity, increases strength from grace entering your life, focuses your mind and heart on Christ, quells mental and emotional turmoil, and promotes a state of deep peace.

JMJ Prayers

The Jesus Prayer

Lord Jesus Christ, Son of God,
have mercy on me, a sinner.

The Hail Mary

Hail Mary, full of grace, the Lord is with thee.
Blessed art thou among women, and blessed is the
  fruit of thy womb, Jesus.
Holy Mary, Mother of God, pray for us sinners now,
  and at the hour of death. Amen.

Petition to St. Joseph

St. Joseph, pray for us.

STEP 10

Practice Physical Precautions

Your spiritual defenses are weakened when you allow yourself to become run down from too little sleep, or too much work and stress. If you are fatigued at the end of an exam week, then take extra precautions against temptations until you restore your physical condition.

If you are going through a period of emotional stress stemming from breaking up with your girlfriend, flunking a class, wrecking your car, fighting with a family member, losing a job, or discovering that your debit card doesn't work because your bank account is empty, then you may be vulnerable to temptation.

Turning to porn to relieve stress will provide a few moments of relief, but will soon increase depression and dependency. At moments of fatigue, stress, and vulnerability you need to make a firm decision to put on the brakes to halt turning to false relief. Instead turn to

Christ in prayer and contact your accountability partner and other friends for fellowship and encouragement.

Too much alcohol or the use of drugs diminishes your ability to make good judgments. Even though marijuana legalization is spreading, don't be foolish by smoking it. Besides filling your lungs with tar, it loosens inhibitions, clouds the mind from discerning a spiritual attack, and dulls the conscience thereby setting you up for a fall.

> Be sober, be watchful. Your adversary the devil prowls around like a roaring lion, seeking some one to devour. – 1 Peter 5:8

Too much idle time and lots of time alone make the struggle against pornography more difficult. Fill idle time with wholesome service, sports, and other activities. You might need to make other prudent changes to your daily and weekly schedule in order to reduce the amount of time you are alone.

If your work requires travel, or if you are on a trip away from home, then be aware that men face additional temptations while on the road. For some reason, many men are prone to lose their moral senses on a trip. Don't lose yours.

I recommend wearing a crucifix or a holy medal during your entire trip, and using holy water liberally in your hotel room. Ask the front desk to block "adult entertainment" in your room. Also, have friends praying for you on your trip. Have your accountability partner call you for an encouragement check-up while you are away and upon your return.

STEP 11

Don't Give Up After a Setback

If you do fall into a sinful setback, be prepared for an onslaught of condemnation. An overwhelming wave of guilt and discouragement can follow in the wake of a setback. The Bible calls Satan "the accuser" of Christians (Revelation 12:10). After a setback Satan will be ready to bombard you with doubts of God's love for you.

St. Paul says to take "the shield of faith, with which you can quench all the flaming darts of the evil one" (Ephesians 6:16). At this point you need to call to mind those scripture verses of God's steadfast love and mercy which you have memorized. Such verses can preserve you from condemnation and despair. (See the verses in the Pure Mind Scripture Memory Kits, especially Psalm 51 and Romans 8:31-39.)

You need to carefully discern between condemnation and conviction. Condemnation from "the accuser" has the effect of driving you away from God. Conviction from the Holy Spirit drives you towards God to find forgiveness and restoration. If you fall, you should certainly not give up the fight. Get to the sacrament of Penance and ask for God's forgiveness. It will always be there for you.

> The steps of a man are from the Lord, and he establishes him in whose way he delights; though he fall, he shall not be cast headlong, for the Lord is the stay of his hand. – PSALM 37:23-24

STEP 12

Hurts That Can Make a Sex Habit Seemingly Impossible to Shake

If your parents were divorced, if your father abandoned your family, if either or both of your parents were alcoholics or drug abusers, if you have been physically, verbally, or sexually abused, if a parent was emotionally unbalanced, if either of your parents failed to demonstrate affection, if you have physical or intellectual limitations that make you feel different from others, or if a friend or family member caused deep and lasting pain in your life, then, for you, Step 12 is the most important step in this booklet.

Hurts deep inside can be tough to shake. Some of us act out in wild and weird ways in an attempt through outward behavior to release hurts that we cannot seem to control on the inside. Others of us bottle up the hurts somewhere deep inside and try to move on with life as though they weren't there – even though these repressed hurts are festering and gnawing at our innermost being.

In my book, *The ABCs of Choosing a Good Wife*, I warn about what I call "the trigger effect." A nice Christian couple gets married expecting marital bliss and then, "boom!" An event unexpectedly triggers suppressed and neglected wounds from past family life. When these buried troubles explode in the midst of a marriage the results are monumental personal *and* marital difficulties.

Dealing with inner wounds and pornography habits *before* marriage is infinitely easier than compounding these struggles by adding marital problems to the mix.

"The trigger effect" can also happen unexpectedly when a guy who is carrying a load of hurts inside sits down to view a little porn for recreation.

Little does he know that viewing pornography releases powerful neurochemicals that stimulate his brain. These brain chemicals give a powerful temporary dose of pleasure *and* have the effect of deadening inner pains. The effect is something like a psychological aspirin that gives temporary relief to those hidden hurts while providing a quick mood boost.

This dual effect of pornography on a man – a blast of pleasure coupled with pain relief – are the ingredients for a seemingly unshakable addiction. When a guy finds that the pleasure and pain relief are very temporary, he goes back for more. As he does, he finds that he needs larger quantities of ever more degrading porn along with frequent masturbation in order to stimulate the same chemical-inducing pleasure and pain relief.

As the habit progresses, the guy feels horrible about himself, and thus the need for the psychological pain relief escalates right along with the frequency and degrading nature of the porn. The mood elevating experience becomes central to the man's life as he struggles with a seemingly impossible-to-shake addiction governing his life.

Pornography, masturbation, alcohol, marijuana, hard drugs, gambling, and extreme risk taking behavior will not heal the hurts inside you. Instead, the following prescription will bring inner healing and peace to your soul.

First and most important is that you honor both of your parents and forgive them, and others, for their shortcomings and injuries to you.

It's a spiritual law to honor our parents if we want things to go well for us in life (Exodus 20:12 & Ephesians 6:2-3). This law is every bit as real and operative in us and in our world as the law of gravity. I guarantee that if you jump out of a ten story building you will get hurt. Disregarding God's law to honor your parents will bring you pain as well.

This doesn't mean that you try to reimagine your parents as perfect persons. They are not. Fathers and mothers on earth aren't perfect; only our Father in heaven is. Imperfections that exist in all parents lead to varying degrees of inner hurts. How you react to these disappointments and injuries will, to a significant degree, determine the course of your life.

A defective type of counseling traces all of our life's problems to our parents' imperfections. This flawed counseling then proceeds to magnify and maintain a negative focus on parental shortcomings. This strategy is more hurtful than helpful.

Your parents aren't perfect and neither are you. That's why we all need to receive divine forgiveness and extend it to others, especially those closest to us. Be warned: if we live with a dishonoring, unforgiving, resentful, and judgmental mindset towards our parents (and other family members), then God will not forgive us.

In the Sermon on the Mount, just after Jesus teaches the "Our Father" prayer, he says, "For if you forgive men their trespasses, your heavenly Father also will forgive you; but if you do not forgive men their trespasses, neither will your Father forgive your trespasses" (Matthew 6:14-15). The Creator who established the law of gravity is also our Lord who runs his universe according to the law of forgiveness. Violate either law and you'll experience hurt.

Addressing Christians, the writer of the Epistle to the Hebrews warns, "See to it that no one fail to obtain the grace of God; that no 'root of bitterness' spring up and cause trouble, and by it the *many* become defiled" (12:15)

If you allow unforgiveness to fester in your heart it will result in a "root of bitterness" growing deep within that will choke all healing, restoring, forgiving, and saving grace. This is a deep trap that *many* Christians fall headlong into. It is one of Screwtape's favorite strategies.

If you have pain within, you need to consciously identify it, confront it, release forgiveness, and seek divine inner healing. Don't seek to escape from it by plunging your heart and mind into a dark virtual reality

A patient priest, or a gifted spiritual director, can help guide you in asking for the Holy Spirit's discovery and healing of hurts. At the very least you need to talk about your hurts to a trusted friend and then ask God out loud for healing grace to be able to extend forgiveness.

Deep resentments, bitterness, and unforgiveness cannot be released by self-effort. Your wounded self is the problem, not the solution. That's why you need to ask God for the power to release the hurts and heal you You may want to go out into the woods and really shout all this to God. He's not hard of hearing, but you really need to get this repressed stuff outside of you. However you decide to do it, get it out with God's grace.

For serious addictions that don't seem to budge, Christian counseling with someone skilled and knowledgeable about the underlying dynamics of sexual addictions can help you heal from the pains that pornography, drugs, or alcohol are being used to medicate. (See *Healing the Wounds of Sexual Addiction*, by Dr. Mark Laaser in the resource section.)

Conclusion

Take one last action step if you are feeling alone, depressed, shameful, or discouraged in your battle with pornography. Watch the movie, *The Passion of the Christ* that Mel Gibson produced, or at least view the scourging scenes. Even if you've seen the movie before watch again the scourging scene where Jesus suffered the merciless lashes of sadistic Roman soldiers. The scourging can be viewed on YouTube.

After viewing the scourging in the *Passion* movie meditate on this passage from the prophet Isaiah. Know for certain that Jesus took all the punishment that we deserved for the sins of the flesh. Keep these scriptures close at hand in the days ahead and grow in the knowledge that Jesus loves you.

> But he was wounded for our transgressions, he was bruised for our iniquities; upon him was the chastisement that made us whole, and with his stripes we are healed.
>
> All we like sheep have gone astray; we have turned every one to his own way; and the LORD has laid on him the iniquity of us all. — Isaiah 53:5-6

APPENDIX

Scripture Memory for a Pure Mind

A man serious about keeping, or restoring, purity will meditate on God's Word regularly: "How can a young man keep his way pure? By guarding it according to thy word." —PSALM 119:9

Romans 12:2

"Do not be conformed to this world but be transformed by the renewal of your mind, that you may prove what is the will of God, what is good and acceptable and perfect."

Comment: A vital part of a life transformation is renewing your mind. The Scriptures, coupled with the power of the Holy Spirit, have the ability to renew your mind from deep within. These internal changes eventually result in an outwardly transformed life.

James 1:14-15

"But each person is tempted when he is lured and enticed by his own desire. Then desire when it has conceived gives birth to sin; and sin when it is full-grown brings forth death."

Comment: There is a process in the growth of sin. It starts with a willful delight in an enticement to sinful desires. Without resistance on our part, the progress towards sin is never halted. The next step is consenting to and yielding to the temptation in a sinful act. Viewing pornography is the commission of a gravely sinful act. For many, the addiction to pornography leads to a desire to commit many of the perverted acts viewed. The wisest way to stop this dreadful process is to resist the very first temptation to sin.

1 Peter 5:8-9

"Be sober, be watchful. Your adversary the devil prowls around like a roaring lion, seeking some one to devour. Resist him, firm in your faith, knowing that the same experience of suffering is required of your brotherhood throughout the world."

Comment: Watch and be on your guard for temptation. Remember the devil often tempts at moments we might not expect, during times of stress, and when we are sick or exhausted. You must firmly resist a spiritual attack with prayer, use of sacramentals, and by recalling to mind words of Scripture.

Galatians 6:7-8

"Do not be deceived; God is not mocked, for whatever a man sows, that he will also reap. For he who sows to his own flesh will from the flesh reap corruption; but he who sows to the Spirit will from the Spirit reap eternal life."

12 Steps to Sexual Purity for Young Men

Comment: Don't be misled by those who say "pornography is no big deal." Sins like pornography have predictable consequences. Sowing pornography into your mind will harm your future marriage and corrupt your spiritual life. Sowing good things in your mind and heart will result in spiritual growth and eternal life.

Proverbs 5:3-5, 8

"For the lips of a loose woman drip honey, and her speech is smoother than oil; but in the end she is bitter as wormwood, sharp as a two-edged sword. Her feet go down to death; her steps follow the path to Sheol ... Keep your way far from her, and do not go near the door of her house."

Comment: Proverbs warns about the flattering and seductive speech of the loose woman. Remember that her "sweet" sounding words are really poison. The wisest way to keep yourself from problems with loose girls is not to go out with them and to avoid places where you know temptation exists.

Psalm 101:3-4

"I will not set before my eyes anything that is base. I hate the work of those who fall away; it shall not cleave to me. Perverseness of heart shall be far from me; I will know nothing of evil."

Comment: Memorize and internalize these verses. Be determined to make them your standard. It might be wise to place these verses on your computer monitor and on top of your TV.

Sirach 21:2

"Flee from sin as from a snake; for if you approach sin, it will bite you. Its teeth are lion's teeth, and destroy the souls of men."

Comment: Pornography is like the venom of a cobra. Flee from it. Those foolish enough to toy with it risk destroying their souls.

Psalm 51:10

"Create in me a clean heart, O God, and put a new and right spirit within me."

Comment: This is King David's prayer asking God to cleanse and renew his heart. God can restore men who have fallen into serious sin. This verse can be wisely used as a daily prayer.

Ephesians 4:22-24

"Put off your old nature which belongs to your former manner of life and is corrupt through deceitful lusts, and be renewed in the spirit of your minds, and put on the new nature, created after the likeness of God in true righteousness and holiness."

Comment: If you really want to live a new life in Christ, then you must quit filling your mind with deceitful lusts. Christ can help you renew your mind, but you must "put off" the corrupt lifestyle.

Philippians 4:8

"Finally, brethren, whatever is true, whatever is honorable, whatever is just, whatever is pure, whatever is lovely, whatever is gracious, if there is any excellence, if there is anything worthy of praise, think about these things."

Comment: You can't fight something with nothing. You can't fight old pornographic images in your mind without having a positive replacement for them.

Sirach 7:36
"In all you do, remember the end of your life, and then you will never sin."

Comment: When tempted to sin, just picture yourself standing before the judgment seat of Christ. Such a sobering focus on the end of your life will help keep you from sin.

Hebrews 4:12
"For the Word of God is living and active, sharper than any two-edged sword, piercing to the division of soul and spirit, of joints and marrow, and discerning the thoughts and intentions of the heart."

Comment: What can cut out the pornographic images implanted deep within your memory? The Word of God has unparalleled power to cleanse you, even in the deepest part of your mind.

1 Corinthians 7:2 & 9
"But because of the temptation to immorality, each man should have his own wife ... But if they cannot exercise self-control, they should marry. For it is better to marry than to be aflame with passion."

Comment: In God's plan, married love-making is a natural outlet for temperate sexual desire. For considering the best ages for marriage, see chapters five and six in *The ABCs of Choosing a Good Wife*. Be advised that marriage will not heal a pornography addiction. You need to get pornography habits out of your life before getting married, or engaged. On the other hand, it may not be wise to unduly postpone getting married. Instead of starting a family, many young men today have a "bucket list" for things desired in their 20's like travel destinations, adventures, achievements and things to accumulate. Here's a big secret: If you want a really fulfilling manly challenge, then pursue marriage and family life.

HELPFUL RESOURCES

www.FamilyLifeCenter.net

Our website has one of the most comprehensive collections of information for Catholic men seeking freedom from pornography addictions.

Since the lists of resources and helpful new ministries are continually updated, frequently check the online resources for "Pornography Help" at www.FamilyLifeCenter.net.

FREE Pure Mind Scripture Program

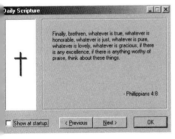

This is an invaluable resource for anyone desiring sexual purity. A different scripture verse will appear each time your computer starts up. This program is frequently recommended by confessors and spiritual advisors. It is available for free download from www.FamilyLifeCenter.net.

Pure Mind Scripture Memory Kits, Vol. I & Vol. II

These memory kits are essential resources for young

men struggling to find freedom from pornography. Each card in the kits has a different Bible verse to memorize for a pure mind. They fit in your pocket so they are always at your fingertips. 20 cards in each kit.

The ABCs of Choosing a Good Wife by Steve Wood

A book for young men filled with time-tested advice for making one of life's most important decisions.

Breaking Free: 12 Steps to Sexual Purity for Men

This booklet is similar to *Young Men Breaking Free* but is geared towards older guys.

Safe Browsers for Smartphones and Tablets

X3watch for the iPhone®, iTouch®, and iPad® is an accountability software program that helps with mobile online integrity. Whenever you browse the Internet and access a questionable site the program will record the name, time, and date the site was visited. A person of your choice (an accountability partner) will receive an email containing all questionable sites visited within the month. Note that the X3watch iPhone application is different from X3watch on Android™ devices. The X3watch browser replaces Safari. This is a slight inconvenience, but if you want accountability on the iPhone this slight inconvenience is well worth it. X3watch also makes a safe browser for Android devices that operates in a slightly different manner. www.X3watch.com.

12 Steps to Sexual Purity for Young Men

Covenant Eyes, like X3watch, offers good accountability browsers for both Apple and Android™ mobile devices. www.covenanteyes.com.

Safe browsers for all your Internet connected devices are necessary for every young man serious about breaking free from a pornography habit.

PC Magazine posts regularly updated reviews of Internet monitoring software for computers and mobile Internet devices. Monitoring software is a necessary tool for a parent or friend assisting you with accountability. www.pcmag.com

Counselors for Pornography Addictions

If you feel that you need a counselor, be sure to choose a person who is specifically trained and experienced in treating the underlying causes of sexual addictions as described in Step 12.

You and/or your parents should read the book, *Healing the Wounds of Sexual Addiction*, by Dr. Mark Laaser before selecting a counselor. It is well worth traveling to obtain a counselor skilled in treating sexual addiction, rather than simply picking someone out of the local phonebook, or off the Internet.

Young Men Breaking Free

Every Young Man's Battle
This DVD presents strategies for victory in the real world of sexual temptation. This is one of the best multi-media tools for teens and college-aged young men seeking to break free from the allure of pornography. It uses powerful personal testimonies, as well as football and military analogies to teach the strategies for winning the battle for sexual purity.

A good way to use this DVD is to invite a few interested friends to view it with you. Afterwards, interested guys can pair-up with an accountability partner.

Discerning Movies, Music, and Video Games
A good website is www.pluggedin.com to begin your evaluation of the things you watch, listen to, and play with. A recommended Plugged In app for your Apple or Android device is available for free download.

Multiple Copies of this Booklet
1 Copy: $3.95
25-99 Copies: $2.95 ea.
100+ Copies: $1.95 ea.

Family Life Center International
2130 Wade Hampton Blvd. • Greenville, SC 29615
www.FamilyLifeCenter.net